how to write a letter

sugar·paper

LOS ANGELES

CLARKSON POTTER/
PUBLISHERS
NEW YORK

how to write a letter

FIND THE WORDS FOR EVERY OCCASION

CHELSEA SHUKOV & JAMIE GROBECKER

ILLUSTRATIONS BY DANIELLE KROLL

To Greg, Owen, and Byrdie
I save every letter you write me.
Those words capture my heart.

———————

To Evan, Kate, and Johnny
Lead with love.
You are my everything.

Contents

INTRODUCTION 08

PART 1: GETTING STARTED 11

letters vs. cards 12
the golden rules 13
picking your paper 14
the essential extras 20
salutations and sign-offs 24
the envelope, please 26

PART 2: SOCIAL CORRESPONDENCE 33

thank you notes 34
letters of love 40
birthdays 48
graduation 56
engagements and marriages 62
babies 70
milestones 76
holidays 82

PART 3: OFFICIAL BUSINESS 91

professional pursuits 92
educational endeavors 100
letters of recommendation 106

PART 4: IT'S COMPLICATED 109

support and sympathy 110
loss 118
separation and divorce 126
apologies 132

PART 5: SUPPLIES 137

ACKNOWLEDGMENTS 140

INDEX 142

B elieve it or not, mail was the preferred method of written communication way back when in the year 2000. It's true—in that year alone, over one million pieces of mail were sent through the United States Postal Service. Shortly thereafter, the internet began to take over, and email quickly overshadowed what became known as "snail mail." The number of letters that people send every year has been on the decline ever since.

But in 2003, when letter writing was becoming a thing of the past, we cofounded a little company you may have heard of called Sugar Paper. We were determined to help people understand that the convenience of emails, and now texts and DMs, are not the same as pouring out your heart and soul onto nice stationery, sealing it with a kiss, and sending it to another to hold in their hands and save forever. After eighteen years of creating paper goods to inspire the letter writer in all of us, we decided to write a book about it.

We are Chelsea Shukov and Jamie Grobecker. Chelsea's love of paper began in grade school with the first Valentine she received in a makeshift mailbox on her desk. She's been putting love in the mail ever since. Jamie's love of paper started in high school with a collection of colorful pens that she used to make passing notes an art form. We've been friends since college and both of us happen to be the type of women who save letters in shoeboxes, still have ticket stubs from first dates, and just can't seem to part with any piece of paper that represents a memory. Growing up, our mothers instilled in each of us the importance of expressing our gratitude on paper, so I guess you could say they started it all.

In the beginning, Sugar Paper was all about the paper and the ink. We knew everything that we needed to know about designing and printing beautiful paper goods and we had become experts in the art of the letterpress. We were making stationery for people who loved paper as much as we did—and were just as sentimental. What we didn't realize was that our clients would ask us so many questions about the "rules" and etiquette for writing the actual messages they wanted to send.

That's when it struck us that not knowing what to say or how to say it for any given occasion was getting in the way of the joy of letter writing.

We wrote this book to answer your questions and give you the confidence to pour your heart out onto a good ol'-fashioned page. Here you'll find stationery basics, sample letters, helpful prompts, and our very best advice for almost every occasion that calls for a note or card. We hope it makes writing easier and inspires you to do so often.

getting started

There are countless occasions to send a card and endless reasons to write a letter. A thoughtful gift deserves a heartfelt thank you; hearing a friend has hit a rough patch calls for at least a few words of support; and falling in love can inspire love notes that would put some of history's greatest romantics to shame. Our favorite excuse is of the just-because variety: Whether it's an inside joke that makes you laugh out loud or reminding a friend that they are wonderful on a totally random day, we're always up for sending a dose of positivity through the mail.

letters vs. cards

With more ways than ever to connect, it's important to choose the right medium for your message.

LETTERS

Letters are the most personal form of correspondence because of the energy and intention they require to compose. Writing a letter is best when you feel compelled to capture and share your thoughts, feelings, and wishes with a specific person. Personal letters are typically written by hand, and business letters are traditionally typed and printed on letterhead.

CARDS

Cards are the most user-friendly form of correspondence because the design helps convey the sentiment and tone. They really come in handy when there is a specific occasion or event such as a birthday or holiday, the purpose is clear, and a concise message will do the trick. A card can have a preprinted message inside or it can be blank; either way, including a handwritten message adds a personal touch.

the golden rules

———

*Whether you feel inspired or etiquette compels you,
we have found a few things that make for
meaningful correspondence nowadays.*

1. Embrace your handwriting. This is what makes any
    note, letter, or card feel personal.

2. Always date your correspondence. Knowing when a
    note was written anchors it in a moment in time.

3. Include a sentiment with your signature. Preprinted
    greeting cards are convenient but can feel
    impersonal.

4. It doesn't have to be a novel. "I love you," for
    example, is only a three-word phrase, but it's one of
    the most powerful.

5. It's never too late to send a letter. Of course, it's best
    if a note arrives in a timely fashion, but it really is the
    thought that counts.

6. Be mindful. If you wouldn't want your children or
    parents to read it, it's probably best not to write it
    down.

picking your paper

Just as there is a time and a place for a certain kind of letter, there is a time and a place for a certain kind of paper.

a note

As a rule of thumb, card stock is used for personalized stationery and cards, and lighter-weight papers are used for letters. Within those two categories you'll find many different weights and textures referred to as the "tooth" of the paper.

There are two types of greeting cards: preprinted and blank. Both have designs on the front, but preprinted cards include text on the inside that makes specific reference to the purpose of the card while blank cards allow you to write any message you want. Next time you're out and about and you see a card that catches your eye, buy it! Collecting cards that speak to you will build your stationery arsenal and ensure you always have the perfect card at the ready.

Boxed stationery is the term used for flat or folded note card sets that include matching envelopes. The sets can be simple solid-colored blank cards, but they typically have a pattern or design and are themed for a specific occasion (like holiday or thank you). There is a huge range of styles within this category but the defining factor here is that they are purchased as-is, without personalization, and are sold in sets so you have more than one on hand at any given time. One way to make boxed stationery feel personal is to select a design featuring the initial of your first or last name.

Personalized stationery is traditionally printed with your initials, monogram, name, or even an illustrated portrait. Think of it as an extension of your personal style, be it formal, casual, playful, modern, or traditional. Ideally, keep two sets on hand: one for business contacts or acquaintances and another for casual communication with friends and family. If you would like to start with a single set, choose a simple design that you feel comfortable sending to anyone, whether to Grandma or the head of HR. We use our personalized stationery for hellos, thank yous, love notes, congratulations, condolences, or any sentiment you want to elevate with a classy touch. For business communication, we often add a note paperclipped on top of the letterhead to add a touch of warmth to the communication.

Letterhead is the thin paper that can be run through a printer and can be folded into a business-size envelope. It's the best choice for professional correspondence. If you run your own business and send letters frequently, you may want to invest in having a logo designed and then printed on letterhead, to be used for formal communication. If your needs are professional in nature but infrequent, you can easily create your own letterhead in a word-processing program. Either way, include your company (if applicable), name, address, telephone number, email, and website. We use letterhead for business communication, letters of recommendation, résumés and cover letters, and official school correspondence. Letterhead adds polish and gravity to any business matters or formal affairs.

a note

It's common now to see letterhead on printer paper, but 100% linen watermarked text-weight paper is the most traditional choice. A watermark lends an air of serious business. Because of its weight and texture, linen watermark paper is more expensive than what you would find in your everyday copy machine.

the essential extras

In addition to the right paper, you'll need writing tools and your address book to make it quick and easy to write and send your card or letter whenever inspiration strikes.

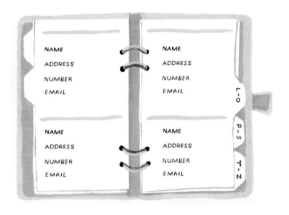

ADDRESS BOOKS

It may seem antiquated, but maintaining a physical address book and keeping it with your letter-writing supplies will make it even easier to send notes to your nearest and dearest when they come to mind. Use a pencil when adding names to your address book so you can make changes as needed. We update our address books every fall in preparation for holiday cards.

writing tools

People are very particular about writing implements. We understand. Each type of pen has a different feel and is an important factor in the overall look of your correspondence. When you use a pen that you like, you are more inclined to write.

BALLPOINT

The ubiquitous pen. There are likely dozens of these around your home, printed with the names of restaurants, dry cleaners, and other brands or businesses. Whether it is retractable or capped, this ink is oil-based and dries almost immediately. Ballpoint pens give a quick and casual look to correspondence.

ROLLERBALL

The smooth operator. The main alternative to a ballpoint pen, this water-based ink flows through a precision tip. It dries quickly but can be smudged just after it hits the page. It has a more elegant appearance than a ballpoint pen.

The artistic choice. These fine-tipped pens are very precise and the water-based ink does not smudge. Along with basic black, they are available in an array of colors. If you would like a signature color for all your social correspondence, choose a felt tip pen in a legible color (dark green, bright pink, gold).

FOUNTAIN PENS

The traditionalist. These classic writing implements have a smooth and easy ink flow thanks to the metal nib and cartridge system, though they can be a bit fussy for the same reasons. Since they are refillable, a good-quality fountain pen can truly last a lifetime.

a note

Ink color counts. While glitter pens and bright colors are fun, black is our go-to. It's the traditional choice and we're traditionalists at heart. Blue ink is the appropriate choice for legal documents and paperwork. With the exception of Valentine's Day cards, red should only be used to make corrections or grade a paper.

salutations and sign-offs

Two things make a letter feel like a letter: the salutation and the sign-off. People have used "dear" as an opener since the mid-fifteenth century, but things have loosened up since then and variations on hello or using only the recipient's name is totally acceptable these days.

When it comes to signing off, there are many options, and whichever you choose will reflect the overall tone of your note. With your family, you may sign every note with "love" but for a note to the head of HR, we recommend something warm, but more formal like "fondly."

Counting the minutes till we meet again

Looking forward to what comes next

Onwards and upwards

To infinity and beyond

I adore you endlessly

With a full heart

With open arms

I love you!

FORMAL

All my best

Best regards

Best wishes

Cordially

Respectfully

Sincerely

With gratitude

With appreciation

TRADITIONAL

Always

As ever

Truly

Take care

Your friend

Cheer

With love

Love

Warmly

Yours

XOXO

a note

*Chelsea goes with "always."
Jamie signs her personal notes
with "xo."*

the envelope, please

In our digital age, we've found that many people have forgotten (or have never even been taught) how to address an envelope. A properly addressed envelope not only ensures that your letter will get to the right place, but it's also your chance to make a good first impression.

When sending a note or card to friends and family, you can use the recipient's full name, first name, or nickname as long as the street address and zip code are correct.

If the envelope for an invitation is addressed to a single person, it means that person alone is invited. If the envelope lists two or more names, those individuals are invited. If it says the family name, you're allowed to bring the kiddos.

how to address an envelope

No matter the occasion, the recipient's address should be centered on the front of the envelope. Start with the recipient's name(s) on the first line, then write the house number and street address on the second line. The third line should have the city, state, and five-digit zip code. Make sure to include your return address on the top left corner (opposite the stamp) or on the flap on the back of the envelope.

a note

When sending professional correspondence, address the envelope with the person's first and last name or you can also use their title if it feels appropriate. If you have any question regarding someone's preferred pronouns, err on the side of caution and simply use their first and last name.

When sending an invitation, the etiquette is to formally address the envelope using a person's or couple's titles and proper address. Write each word out fully—that means absolutely no abbreviations. For invitations, we prefer calligraphy or hand-addressing envelopes with a pen.

TRADITIONAL

Dr. and Mrs Morgan Fines
1749 Ensley Avenue
Los Angeles, California 90024

FORMAL

Mrs Claire Fines
1749 Ensley Avenue
Los Angeles, California 90024

CASUAL

the Fines Family
1749 Ensley Avenue
Los Angeles, California 90024

A return address serves two purposes: It allows for the post office to return your letter in the event the recipient's address is incorrect or the postage is insufficient; it also lets the recipient know who the letter or package is from, providing them with your address should they like to send a reply.

The two most common places for a return address are the upper left-hand corner of the front of the envelope or on the back flap, the former being used most often for casual and professional correspondence, and the latter for personalized stationery, invitations, and holiday cards.

If it's social correspondence, you can choose to include your full name, first or last name, first initial and last name, family, or nickname. If this is professional correspondence, it's best to include the name of your business and full name.

One of the biggest reasons people do not follow through with sending letters is that they don't have a stamp handy. Easy fix: Buy two sheets from your neighborhood post office to have on hand so you're never in a pinch. Stamps add to the beauty of the envelope and many designs are limited edition. Consider your stamp a piece of art, and the final touch to heartfelt communication.

For holiday greetings, invitations, or any correspondence that you would like treated with care, ask the clerk at the post office to add a postmark by hand. Choosing to have your stamps hand-canceled adds an old-fashioned touch that beautifully marks the stamp with the date and place of origin. Otherwise, most mail is run through a machine to cancel stamps to prevent reuse and the process can damage an envelope and/or its contents. Not all post offices offer this service, but we have found that there is usually one nearby that does.

social correspondence

This is the good stuff. These are the just-because notes, celebratory wishes, and exciting hellos that are written with love, sent through the mail, and arrive on someone's doorstep like a little ray of paper sunshine.

thank you notes

personalized stationery, boxed stationery, or a card

Even if the only letter writing you ever do is doling out thank
you notes, then our job here is done. When someone has
given you a gift, done something for you, or gone out of their
way to show you kindness, acknowledge their generosity and
efforts with a thanks. Instead of opening with the standard
"Thank you for the [fill in the blank]," which can feel stiff
and formulaic, our best advice is to start your note with the
word *you*. It opens a world of possibilities. For example, "You
shouldn't have!" or "You are the most thoughtful person I
know." Then, say thank you. It works like a charm when you
need help getting the gratitude flowing.

finding the

RIGHT WORDS

———

YOU REMEMBERED!

YOU SHOULDN'T HAVE.

YOU ARE SO THOUGHTFUL.

WORDS CANNOT EXPRESS MY GRATITUDE.

YOUR THOUGHTFUL GIFT . . .

I'M SO INSPIRED BY YOU.

YOU'VE CHANGED MY LIFE.

YOU ARE WONDERFUL, GENEROUS, AND KIND.

I WILL NEVER FORGET . . .

THANK YOU.

Although the etiquette books will tell you it's important to write a thank you note the day you receive a gift, we feel that it's never too late for gratitude.

Dear Mom and Dad,

You are the greatest parents ever.
I know I'm biased but it's true. As
a little girl, I loved your etching
that hung in our dining room. It
was my favorite piece of art in
the house. I can't believe you
were able to part with it, but I'm
delighted you did. You must have
known how much it means to me. I
can't wait to hang it in the living
room. Thank you for giving it to
me; I will give it a good home.
I love you.

Always,

Chelsea

Everyone loves a party, but rarely do we stop to think about all the effort that actually goes into throwing one. For gracious hosts, we like to call out our favorite memory or the very best part of the event. We always make sure to include a compliment.

Dear Katie,

You are the ultimate host. We drank rosé all day (and night!) surrounded by the prettiest pink décor. I've never met anyone who loves pink more than you! I couldn't think of a better way to celebrate the first weekend of summer. Looking forward to more sunny days with you!

xo,

Jamie

Our favorite thank yous are the ones we send that
acknowledge someone for the good they bring to our
lives rather than just the literal goods. These notes are
written to the people you love and admire to let them
know how much they mean to you. If you've never
written a note like this, now's your chance.

Seth,

You are—hands down—one of the most amazing humans on this planet. You are so generous with your time and encouragement, and I am a better person for having met you. Thank you for always cheering me on and for telling me the truth when I need to hear it. It's rare to find a friend like you. I appreciate you more than you will ever know.

Always,
Chelsea

letters of love

absolutely anything goes

The idea of writing a love letter might be intimidating, but no one is expecting Romeo and Juliet–level prose. The truth is that notes of affection can take many forms. Whether it is a letterpress card inscribed with a sonnet or "I love you" scribbled on scrap paper and stuck to the refrigerator, these are the notes we hold most dear—no swirly calligraphy or wax seal required.

When it comes to love notes, vulnerability is one of the keys to connection. You may be hesitant to put your feelings on paper, but when you do, they become the most meaningful keepsakes of your life. Don't overthink it.

finding the

RIGHT WORDS

———

I AM SO GRATEFUL FOR YOU . . .

YOU'VE CHANGED THE WAY THAT I LOOK AT . . .

HAVING YOU IN MY LIFE MEANS . . .

I WILL ALWAYS REMEMBER THAT TIME WHEN . . .

WHEN I THINK ABOUT YOU, I AM FILLED WITH . . .

I AM SO LUCKY TO KNOW YOU.

I ADORE YOU.

I LOVE YOU.

During the early days of feeling absolutely smitten, you can pour your heart out onto the page. As love grows, you may not feel compelled to express yourself with the same passion, but you can always reaffirm your feelings, celebrate something about your partner, or touch on a special memory. When you come across these years later, you will be glad you did.

a note

P.S. stands for postscriptum, which means "after writing" in Latin and is used to add another message after a letter has been written and signed. Writing the actual phrase "post scripta" or P.S. can be traced to England in the 1500s, but people have been tacking on one last thought to their correspondence since the days of Tacitus (56–120 AD). To start a letter over would have been a waste of papyrus.

Greg,

I know it's only been a few hours since your plane took off, but as I sit here without you, I can't stop thinking about you. Thank you for the dreamy weekend. I had long since given up on the idea that someone would open the car door for me, and actually stand up when I excused myself from the table. Or that someone so considerate could also be so smart and good looking. Lucky me. I love every minute we spend together.

I adore you.
Always,
Chelsea

Greg,

Today I love you more than
yesterday and less than I will
tomorrow. The first time I heard
that we were newly married. Now,
we're up to our ears in diapers.
Happy Anniversary.

Yours Always,
Chelsea

Anniversary cards are as special and important as the love notes written in the early days of romance. And for most, they are also very different. Like relationships, over time, the sentiments may shift from "All I do is dream of you the whole night through," to "All I do is dream of the day we get to sleep past 6:15 a.m." As the years go on, be sure to date your card or letter, reference the stage of life you are in, and reflect this moment in time.

Letters acknowledging and celebrating friendship will always hold a special place in our hearts. Technology has truly made it so much easier to stay in touch with texts and social media, but there is no substitute for the experience of sifting through a stash of paper ephemera and striking gold.

While it's simply good manners to send thank yous and greeting cards to friends, it's the out-of-the-blue, I-am-so-lucky-to-know-you notes that will be cherished forever.

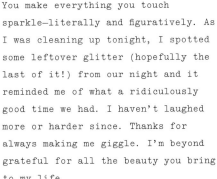

Dear Jamie,

You make everything you touch
sparkle—literally and figuratively. As
I was cleaning up tonight, I spotted
some leftover glitter (hopefully the
last of it!) from our night and it
reminded me of what a ridiculously
good time we had. I haven't laughed
more or harder since. Thanks for
always making me giggle. I'm beyond
grateful for all the beauty you bring
to my life.

Always,
Chelsea

birthdays

a card

There are two types of birthday people in this world: those who love celebrating each passing year as a miraculous milestone, and those who prefer to subscribe to a business-as-usual take on the whole thing (you can guess where we stand on the issue). Whatever your stance, everyone appreciates a card—they just may not want a singing telegram delivered to their office.

a note

Always note the milestone, shower the birthday celebrant with compliments, and include wishes for the future.

finding the

RIGHT WORDS

———

HERE'S TO ANOTHER YEAR FILLED WITH . . .

I HOPE THIS YEAR BRINGS YOU . . .

I AM SO GLAD YOU WERE BORN.

I HOPE YOU SPEND YOUR DAY . . .

MAY ALL YOUR BIRTHDAY WISHES
COME TRUE.

Kids are most often on the receiving end of the sign-and-send greeting card scenario. Whenever possible, add personal messages to their cards by acknowledging who they are at this moment in their lives, what they love, and reinforcing your relationship. These are the cards that wind up in the attic that will fill a full-grown adult with delight.

Happy Birthday, Byrdie!

You used to be the most amazing
seven-year-old I knew, and now
you're the most amazing eight-year-
old! I hope the year ahead is full
of many magical memories, sparkling
potions, and backyard adventures!
Hooray for you!

Love always,
Auntie Jammer

Kirby,

And to think just a year ago we were
in Mexico celebrating with tacos
and very fancy, very sophisticated
tequila beneath the stars (or was
that the table?). You have a special
way of bringing out the joy in
everyone and I'm so excited to be
along for the ride. Thank goodness
we (especially you!) survived that
vacation so that we can be here today
celebrating your latest trip around
the sun. Here's to the best one yet.

Salud!
Jamie

When it comes to writing a birthday message to a friend, anything goes. From heartfelt and sentimental to utterly silly, or something in between, these notes are some of the most satisfying to write, read, and save forever and ever.

It's our nearest and dearest who are often on the receiving end of a phone call or a quick HBD text. If you speak frequently, it might feel unnecessary to send something through the mail. We say this is even more reason to do so. You may find that what you choose to write in a card is much different from what you talk about at the dinner table. They'll say you shouldn't have, but they will sure be glad that you did.

Dear Grammy,

I bet you've been waiting by the mailbox for your annual birthday card for the last 364 days! You didn't think that I would let you down on your 87th birthday, did you? Well, here it is! Happy birthday! I hope that today is the best day ever and that this year is full of joy, happiness, and winning lottery tickets.

Always your favorite,
Chelsea

graduation

a card

Hard work deserves a big pat on the back and most certainly a card. Graduating from nursery school, elementary school, middle school, high school, college, or a postgraduate program are not only achievements, but they are also coming-of-age moments. Even if you were not invited to attend the ceremony, still send a card. There is no such thing as too many well wishes or words of encouragement.

finding the

RIGHT WORDS

———

BRAVO!

WHAT AN IMPRESSIVE ACHIEVEMENT.

YOU SHOULD BE SO PROUD.

GOODBYE SCHOOL, HELLO WORLD!

CAN'T WAIT TO SEE WHAT YOUR FUTURE HOLDS.

YOU DESERVE ALL THIS SUCCESS AND MORE.

I'M CHEERING FOR YOU TODAY AND ALWAYS.

YOU DID IT!

Graduating from high school is a big deal. With their secondary school behind them, graduates are truly embarking on their journeys to adulthood—plus, it's a rite of passage. If someone gave you a piece of advice or a quote that has guided you, this is a perfect time to pass it on.

Maddie,

You did it! All of the early mornings, late nights, final exams, heavy backpacks, practice sessions, hard work, and dedication has led to this. Happy graduation. You should be so proud—we certainly are!

Love you!
Auntie Jamers and the fam

Scott,

This day has finally come. You're a
doctor! It's official. We know how
incredibly devoted you have been to
this dream, and it's been inspiring
to see you make it come true.
We cannot wait to see where your
brilliant mind, tireless work ethic,
and boundless energy take you next.
We love you and couldn't be more
proud.

Love always,
Chelsea and Greg

Like high school, college graduation signifies the end of one chapter in someone's life and the beginning of another. Grads deserve to celebrate this moment and the acknowledgment of their academic achievements has been well earned.

engagements and marriages

a card

When a couple decides to get hitched, it's a public declaration of their love and devotion to each other. As the couple lays the foundation for their future, it's an especially wonderful time to celebrate them and let them know you're cheering them on every step of the way.

finding the

RIGHT WORDS

———

HERE'S TO A LIFETIME OF LOVE

AND HAPPINESS.

GOOD THINGS ARE COMING YOUR WAY.

CHAMPAGNE ALL AROUND!

HERE'S TO THE MOST PERFECT COUPLE

WE KNOW.

YOU'RE MADE FOR EACH OTHER.

News of an engagement fills the air with hope, optimism, and love—it's also kind of a big deal. Notes of congratulations for this wonderful moment in a couple's life should do the same. Whether or not you think you will be invited to the wedding, send a congratulatory engagement card if you feel so inclined.

Quinn and David,

From the moment Quinn cut in
front of you in the ice cream
line, we knew you two were meant
for each other. Two years later,
you're engaged. Wishing you a long
life full of love, luck, health,
happiness, and an endless supply
of Jeni's Ice Cream.

Here's to true love!
Chelsea

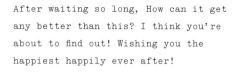

Allie and Sean,

After waiting so long, How can it get
any better than this? I think you're
about to find out! Wishing you the
happiest happily ever after!

xo,
Chelsea and Jamie

We would be willing to bet that most cards that newlyweds receive are going to be saved, so put the extra effort in to make yours a keeper. Start with a beautiful card and include a message that could only be from you. If you are unable to attend, send your card and gift anytime, but ideally after you have RSVP'd with regrets and before the big day. If you are attending the wedding, it's perfectly acceptable to send your card and gift after the event so that you can include special details.

Weddings are celebrations of love, so there's no need to fill cards with weighty words and heavy sentiments—be sincere without being too serious.

Dear Ellen and Casey,

It's been a few weeks since your
wedding, but I am still thinking
about your beautiful vows. Witnessing
the deep, true love and appreciation
you have for each other was an honor.
May the feelings you have now only
grow stronger over time.

All our love,
The Shukovs

the wedding present

THANK YOU

———

*For every wedding gift received, a handwritten thank you note is a must.
Technically, couples have one year from their wedding date to send
their thanks, but, as they say, time flies! After a wedding, the number
of notes you will need to write can feel overwhelming. There are a
few ways to tackle wedding gift thank yous.*

Here's our best advice:

Write the note immediately after opening the gift.

OR

Write the note immediately after using
the gift for the first time.

OR

Create a spreadsheet with columns for the gift, the
giver, and notes or impressions. Be sure to mark
whom you have sent notes to.

babies

a card

There are so many reasons to celebrate, and a new baby might be the cutest one of all. As moms with two kids each, we know all about wanting to celebrate and capture those very first moments so you can bottle them up. This phase of life is full of emotion and the notes that someone receives around these events are automatic keepsakes that they will treasure forever.

Welcoming a child can take many paths—some are incredibly smooth (surprising even!) and others fraught with challenges. Whether the child is biological, delivered via surrogate, adopted, or any other modern miracle, what matters most is that a new person has arrived. Focus on the joys of a new addition and a growing family and skip any references to how it may have happened.

finding the

RIGHT WORDS

———

CHERISH THESE FIRST NEW DAYS TOGETHER.

CONGRATULATIONS ON YOUR BEAUTIFUL CHILD.

WE ARE SO EXCITED FOR YOUR
GROWING FAMILY.

WE CAN'T WAIT TO MEET THE NEWEST MEMBER OF
YOUR FAMILY.

SENDING ALL THE LOVE IN OUR HEARTS
TO YOU AND YOURS.

HELLO TO OUR NEW FAVORITE PERSON.

WE LOVE THEM ALREADY!

Whether a baby shower is four people or forty, the reason for the gathering is personal, so your letter to the parent(s)-to-be should be too. For first-time parent(s), so much excitement and anticipation for the whole new world is awaiting them. For those with children already, it may seem like they have done it all before, but it's still a time full of wonder and excitement.

Emily,

Your little one is almost here! You
have always been the most wonderful,
nurturing, present, fun-loving, and
patient friend, so naturally, you are
going to be an incredible mom. We
cannot wait to meet your tiny miracle
and see you in action. Know that we
are here for you and your growing
family in any way you may need—all
you have to do is call.

xo,

Jamie and Chelsea

Dear Ellen and Matt,

We were over the moon to hear the good news! Our hearts have been full ever since. Here is a little something for Otis. We hope it will bring good health and pure happiness.

Sincerely,
Jamie and Chelsea

P.S. We tucked in a little something for big sister, Irene.

Word of a new healthy, happy baby travels fast. It's ideal to send a card and/or gift promptly after hearing the news. The first few days, weeks, and even months of having an infant at home can be a blur and feel quite isolating for parents, so receiving your warm wishes in the mail not only brightens their day but is also a happy reminder of the outside world.

Although babies are the most common new additions, a child of any age can join a family through adoption. This is an especially sweet reason to send a card and/or gift and one that not everyone thinks to celebrate so your thoughtful note will mean even more to the recipient.

milestones

personal stationery, boxed stationery, or a card

There are some moments in life that deserve recognition you will never find preprinted on a calendar: moving into a new apartment after years of living with roommates, buying a first home, inking a dream deal, leaving a stifling job, starting a new business. When someone you care about takes a scary leap or checks off a major goal on their list, take the time to acknowledge it. It shows how well you know them, and lets them know you care. Keep your notes of acknowledgment lighthearted and lively so the recipient feels like they just received a high five, and remember: Celebrate all victories, big and small.

finding the

RIGHT WORDS

———

GOOD LUCK.

YOU HAVE EARNED THIS.

YOU DESERVE IT.

YOU'VE GOT THIS.

ALL YOUR HARD WORK HAS PAID OFF.

WISHING YOU ALL THE SUCCESS
IN THE WORLD.

I CAN'T WAIT TO SEE WHAT HAPPENS NEXT.

Moving can be complex: On one hand, there's a world of possibilities ahead, and on the other, there's something being left behind. In any case, it's a big change. Whether someone is settling into a new apartment, relocating across the country, or buying their first house, receiving a card in the mail at their new address will put a smile on their face.

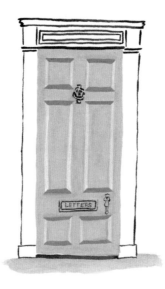

To the new resident
of Montana Avenue!

Trevor and Jules, you looked for
ages and ages and finally found the
perfect place to call your own.
I can't wait for game night—I'll
bring the Bananagrams! Can't wait to
celebrate with you.
Congrats!

xo,
Jamie

At the start of any new endeavor, it feels especially good to know that someone is in your corner. This is the time for confidence boosters and unbridled encouragement as they enter a new phase of their career.

```
Laurel,

You are a BOSS. Literally. They are
so lucky to have you.
Congrats, my friend.

Love,
Chelsea
```

It's not every day that all of someone's hard work pays off. Recognizing someone for their accomplishments or reaching a long-standing goal lets them know that you've been paying attention all along the way.

Keri,

You are such an inspiration. You saw what you wanted and made it happen and I couldn't be more proud of you.

Congratulations!
Jamie

holidays

a card

We consider holidays to be the gateway to all card sending and letter writing. They are the most obvious case for sending a card, so preprinted greeting cards are widely available. Once you see how easy mailing a card can be and hear how good a simple gesture can make someone else feel, you'll be hooked.

finding the

RIGHT WORDS

———

WISHING YOU A SEASON FULL OF

LOVE AND LAUGHTER.

MAY YOU HAVE JOY IN YOUR HEART AND HAPPINESS

IN YOUR HOME THIS SEASON AND ALWAYS.

WISHING YOU A HAPPY HOLIDAY AND

A JOYFUL NEW YEAR.

WARMEST HOLIDAY WISHES.

HAPPY HOLIDAYS FROM OUR FAMILY TO YOURS.

There are plenty of holidays to celebrate with paper throughout the year. People have been exchanging homemade valentines since the fifteenth century. Today, we send cards to family and friends for Valentine's Day and all the rest: Halloween, Easter, Mother's Day, Father's Day—you name it.

Jessica,

Happy Valentine's Day to the girl
who just gets me. I'm so lucky
to call you my friend.

Always,
Chelsea

Dad,

Being with you is my favorite thing
to do. Thank you for making me the
person I am today.

All my love,
Jamie

Our attitude is always the more the merrier, especially when it comes to holiday cards. Sending season's greetings came into vogue in 1843 when Sir Henry Cole decided to buck the tradition of an annual long-form letter and sent out custom printed greeting cards to his thousand closest friends instead. Today, holiday cards keep us connected to our nearest and dearest and serve as a line of communication between us and those we rarely see. When you hold a holiday card in your hands, it's a tiny reminder that someone out there is thinking of you wherever they may be.

Let your holiday card be a reflection of your family's unique spirit. You might be formal and choose a very classic, letterpress design or perhaps you prefer to keep things laidback and send a playful photograph. If you have them, include a photo of your kid(s) (yes, pets count).

a note

Try to place your order just after Halloween to allow plenty of time for you to receive your cards and send them out just after Thanksgiving.

how to pull off a perfect holiday card in

six easy steps

———

1. Find your style: Decide what you would like the overall vibe to look like and then select accordingly.

2. If you plan on including a photo, take the photo in September so you can place your order early.

3. When including a photo, design your card around it to give the card a cohesive, intentional look and feel.

4. Buffer your order. There are always a few friends that come close to being forgotten—extra cards make sure they'll be included.

5. Holiday cards are timely and should be sent out as such. Aim to be finished by the first week of December.

6. If you're running late, opt for a New Year's card.

When sending a holiday card from your business, choose a streamlined design or create something custom that reflects your brand. Often, professional holiday cards have secular themes such as peace and love with wintry designs. It's important that your choice reflect inclusivity.

official business

Time to get down to business. Professional correspondence includes the carefully formatted and thoughtfully worded letters to prospective schools, programs, employers, and clubs and organizations. In many cases, your letter will be the recipient's first impression of you. Let's make it a good one.

professional pursuits

letterhead, personal stationery, or a card

Career paths may take several twists and turns and good
etiquette always helps to get ahead. In all your professional
communications, dot your *i*'s and cross your *t*'s—literally!
Proper grammar and correct spelling are essential. Making
specific references to the company and your conversation
shows that you pay attention to details. And make sure to spell
everyone's name right. As the founders of a small company, we
have received notes from many candidates over the years and
they carry a lot of weight in our hiring process.

It may not always be the higher-ups who need impressing; a
well-timed, well-intentioned note has the power to strike the
right chord with esteemed colleagues, would-be collaborators,
and key team members.

finding the

RIGHT WORDS

———

THIS IS AN AMAZING OPPORTUNITY

BECAUSE . . .

I AM WELL-SUITED FOR THIS BECAUSE . . .

I WOULD BE A GOOD FIT FOR THIS

BECAUSE . . .

TO ME, REALIZING THIS DREAM

WOULD MEAN . . .

THANK YOU FOR YOUR TIME.

THANK YOU FOR YOUR CONSIDERATION.

I HOPE TO HEAR FROM YOU.

letterhead

In the digital age, most postinterview thank yous are sent via email and wind up in the HR department's in-box. However, when a candidate sends a timely note through the mail, it lands on the addressee's desk and can't be ignored. If you want to stand out, we recommend sending a handwritten thank you the same day as the interview. When your note arrives a day or two later, it serves as an additional reminder that you are a great (and thoughtful) candidate.

Dear Chelsea and Jamie,

Thank you so much for meeting
with me last Thursday. Time is a
precious resource and I'm grateful
for yours. More than anything,
I would love the opportunity to
bring my passion for authentic
storytelling and marketing to
your team. I sincerely hope
you consider me for this role.

All my best,

Meredith

Dear Chelsea,

When I started at this company three years ago, I knew it was an amazing opportunity, but I had no idea how lucky I was. Your sharp focus, impeccable standards, and professionalism have helped shape my career. Even though I am no longer part of your team, I will be taking all that I have learned from you with me and for that I am forever grateful. Thank you so much for all your time and guidance. I hope our paths cross again in the future.

Sincerely,
Joanna

letterhead or a card

Whatever the circumstances may be, it's always ideal to leave a job on a high note. Think of your exit letter as being an opportunity to tie up your working experience with your former employer with a big, pretty bow. Express your appreciation, share what you have learned, and keep your language professional. Remember the good times and leave it at that.

letterhead, personal stationery, or a card

In professional circles, the exchange of ideas and information is natural, but that doesn't mean it should go unacknowledged. No matter how busy your daily agenda may be, take a moment to say thank you to those who are generous and forthcoming with their expertise, information, and address books.

Dear Kellie,

You have a way of making the most
complex logistical issues seem like a
walk in the park! Thank you for being
a thought partner. I am so fortunate
to have you on speed dial.

IOU,
Chelsea

educational endeavors

letterhead, personal stationery, or a card

From preschool to grad school, the school application process is notoriously competitive. Admissions directors receive piles of applications every year and a good cover letter aims to get them interested in learning more about you. This is your opportunity to share what makes you unique.

letterhead

Along with the application itself and your letters
of recommendation, a dynamic cover letter is your
chance to get your application to stand out in a sea of
candidates. Let them know why you're a perfect fit for the
program. Some schools only accept digital applications,
but for those that accept physical applications, including
a cover letter on letterhead will show your commitment
and attention to detail.

November 08, 2020

Mrs. Parker
Marigold University
123 Flower Field Road
Sonoma, CA 95476

Dear Mrs. Parker,

I am writing today with my application to Marigold University. After exploring many different schools and educational paths, discovering your unique philosophy truly resonated with me.

Your esteemed school has cultivated generations of original thinkers and groundbreaking talents and I hope to follow in their footsteps. Where many places of higher education strive for sameness, Marigold inspires individuality. I have always worked tirelessly

to make my own way and with my passion for
entrepreneurial pursuits, thus I feel that I would thrive
at your institution.

Nowhere else values curiosity, collaboration, diversity,
intellect, and creativity more than Marigold, and that
is why I aspire to become a Goldie.

Enclosed you will find my formal application,
high school transcripts, essays, and three letters
of recommendation. It would be an honor to be
accepted and I am deeply grateful for your time and
consideration.

Sincerely,

Quincy Taylor

Dear Professor Cooke,

What an honor it was to be able
to sit with you last week for my
admissions interview. After touring
and researching West Coast University
for the past year and a half, having
the opportunity to hear your insights
into the academic environment, campus
culture, and life as an esteemed
alumna was incredibly affirming.
I am certain that these hallowed
halls are the place for me. It would
truly be a dream come true to begin
the next chapter of my education
at WCU. I feel strongly that I have
what it takes and I hope you and the
admissions department see it too.
Thank you so much for your time.

With appreciation,
Owen Bennett

letterhead or a card

Applying to school requires several steps, including a campus tour, a formal application, complete with letters of recommendation, and a one-on-one interview. Once this interview is over, applicants have one last chance to make an impression: the postinterview thank you note. Making the extra effort to remind them of who you are could make all the difference.

letters of recommendation

When applying to school, interviewing for a new job, or joining a private club, letters of recommendation are usually a part of the application process. Because we aren't asked to write this type of letter every day, writing one can feel daunting. Before you set out to write your recommendation, collect your thoughts. You will need to provide details about the individual or family and the words you will write will be important as to how they are perceived. Most importantly: Know your audience. Let the tone of your letter follow that of the person, establishment, or organization that will be reading it.

a note

When someone goes to the effort of helping you out, remember to say thank you. When someone writes a formal letter of recommendation, arranges a meeting with the headmaster, or puts in a good word with the school board, consider writing a thoughtful card and sending a small gift as a token of your appreciation. The accompanying note can be short and sweet, since it will be very clear what the thank you is for.

Dear Mrs. Winward,

I am writing this letter to you as a personal reference for Kate Grobecker. Kate is a third-grade student at Lovely Day School and the daughter of our close friends, Jamie and Evan. Kate is a darling little girl who comes from a family with great values. She is sweet, well-mannered, and kind. Kate's curiosity and sincere nature would be a great addition to next year's fourth-grade class. I have known Jamie and Evan since we met fifteen years ago in college and I am confident that the Grobecker family would be a great addition to your school. I cannot recommend them highly enough.

Sincerely,
Chelsea Shukov

it's complicated

Life isn't always birthday parties and engagement dinners. It has its gray skies, curveballs, and heartbreaks, too. Our friends and family are there for us through it all. While you may feel unsure about reaching out during turbulent times, we believe it is always the right thing to do. The beauty of sending a card or note is that you are able to be there for them while respecting their privacy and space.

support and sympathy

stationery, boxed stationery, or a card

When times are tough, even the toughest need empathy and compassion. So, when it seems that a friend, loved one, or anyone who plays a valuable part in your life may be going through something challenging, it's even more important to show up for them. Taking a moment to write a heartfelt note can make a world of difference, even if you don't know exactly what to say.

finding the

RIGHT WORDS

———

I AM THINKING OF YOU.

I'M SO SORRY.

I AM HERE IF YOU WANT TO TALK ABOUT IT.

YOU CAN COUNT ON ME.

I LOVE YOU.

I CAN'T IMAGINE WHAT YOU'RE GOING THROUGH . . .

When we hear that someone is having a difficult time, it's easy to assume they have a lot going on or don't want to be bothered. Instead of pulling back, lean in. It's easy to shy away from painful subjects or touchy conversations, but when you send a card, you let someone know that you are there for them and available to talk about the tough stuff on their terms.

Dear Jen,

You have been on my mind nonstop. You have always inspired those around you with your grace and strength and now is no different. I would love to talk or come by whenever feels best to you. Please know I am sending all my love and am here to help in any way that I can.

Yours Truly,
Jamie

Anne,

I know your situation is
unpredictable, but our friendship
is not. Whether it's company for a
doctor's appointment in the middle of
the day or someone to talk to in the
middle of the night, you can always
count on me. I am here to help in
any way I can.

I love you.

Chelsea

A life-threatening diagnosis or major injury is something that no one should face alone. Be there for your friend or loved one in the same way you would like them to be there for you. A card, thoughtful gift, or supportive act is always appropriate. The months or even years following can be isolating and difficult, so staying in touch can shine warmth and light on dark times.

One of the most sensitive and private matters in a person or couple's life is their path to parenting. At its best, it's easy and uneventful until the day their child is born. At its most difficult, it's a complicated and lengthy process with no guarantees, full of medical complexities and challenges that can cause stress physically, emotionally, socially, and financially. When these circumstances arise, nothing is more important than support from trusted confidants. The best thing you can do in these unique circumstances is respect your friend's privacy while offering to support them in whatever way that works best for them.

Fiona,

It was so good to catch up the other
night—you've been on my mind ever
since. Thank you for trusting me
with all the ups and downs of your
journey. There's no way for me to
know what this must be like for you
and John, but if you ever want to
talk—or not talk and hike, shop, or
go to a yoga class—I'm here for you.

Yours always,
Jamie

loss

stationery, boxed stationery, or a card

When someone you care about has lost a loved one, it often feels impossible to find the right words to say. Don't let this stop you from showing up. If you did not know the deceased, focus on your friend or what you know about your friend's relationship to their loved one. Avoid labeling their feelings for them: Grief is a complex and delicate issue and everyone deals with it in their own unique way. Sincerely acknowledging the loss and offering your condolences can be enough.

finding the

RIGHT WORDS

———

I AM TRULY SORRY FOR YOUR LOSS.

I WILL ALWAYS REMEMBER . . .

YOU ARE ALWAYS IN MY THOUGHTS.

I'M NOT ENTIRELY SURE WHAT TO SAY
EXCEPT THAT I CARE ABOUT YOU.

I KNOW THIS IS PAINFUL AND I
AM HERE FOR YOU.

Regardless of the circumstances, losing your spouse or partner is not only devastating but destabilizing. In addition to the initial emotions of heartache, immense sadness, and grief, there are immediate and intense shifts in day-to-day life. During this time, there are few more important sentiments than letting your friend know that they are not alone.

Dear Miranda,

I am so saddened to hear of Michael's
passing. I cannot imagine how
difficult this must be for you. He had
the warmest smile and biggest heart.
Like all who knew him, I feel truly
lucky to have been able to call him a
friend. During this time and always,
please know that you and your family
are in my thoughts. If you need any
help whatsoever - I'm here. I want to
support you in any and all ways that
I can.

With all my love,
Chelsea

With an unimaginable tragedy such as the loss of a child, there are no words that will take away the pain, but it is important to send a message of support no matter what. Letters of condolence, flower deliveries, or any heartfelt gestures of support can bring comfort to the parents, reminding them their child was greatly loved.

Dear Megan and Sam,

There are no words to express the great depths of my sympathies during this tragic time. Alex will never be forgotten. Anytime we see a rainbow we will think of her. Your family is in my thoughts and heart today and always.

Yours truly,
Jamie

We are often asked if it is appropriate to send a condolence card to a friend when they have lost a family member if you did not know the deceased. Our answer is absolutely. Losing someone is never easy, and any support is always appreciated.

Dear Rebecca,

I am so sorry to hear of your
father's passing. Though I never
had the pleasure of meeting him, I
know you two were incredibly close.
Please know I am thinking of you
and your family during this time.
If you need anything at all - a ride
to the airport or for me to pick up
your mail while you are out of town
- please don't hesitate to ask. I am
here for you.

Always,
Chelsea

Charlie,

I'm so sorry to hear about Peaches.
I know how much you loved your sweet
cuddle buddy. She will be missed
around the neighborhood.

Thinking of you,
The Shukovs

a note

Pets
Animals hold a very special place in people's hearts.
After the loss of a pet, sending a short note or even a
text in a timely fashion that expresses your condolences
and warmly acknowledges their special bond will
mean so much.

separation and divorce

stationery, boxed stationery, or a card

Even under the best circumstances, separations and divorces
are difficult. Though some couples may see eye to eye on
the decision and others may fight every step of the way, the
realities of splitting up involve dismantling a shared life, sorting
through a myriad of emotions, and, eventually, reimagining
a future that likely looks very different. When writing your
note, be clear, be concise, and offer your presence and support
without inserting yourself into private matters. Handle with
care.

finding the

RIGHT WORDS

———

SOMETIMES GOOD CHOICES ARE THE
HARDEST ONES TO MAKE.

TELL ME HOW I CAN HELP.

I'M HERE FOR YOU NO MATTER WHAT.

IS NOW A GOOD TIME FOR A GLASS OF WINE?

A messy divorce is the very worst kind. No matter how tempting it may be to fire off all the reasons and ways an ex was absolutely wrong, invest in words that lift your friend's spirits, confidence, strength, and hope.

Carly,

I've wanted to call, but I wasn't sure exactly what to say. I'm sorry you are going through such a tricky time. Whenever you're up for getting together or want a distraction, please let me know and I'll be right there. And no matter what, remember that you are so loved by so many—especially me.

Always,
Chelsea

Even if things seem like they are for the best, it doesn't mean that they are necessarily easy. Sending messages of love and support even when things look perfectly fine from the outside is a good way to let someone know you care and are there for them in both the good times and bad. Your note may be the open door they are looking for.

```
Courtney,

You are the epitome of grace
and strength.
If you ever want to talk, I am
here for you.

With love,
Jamie
```

The decision to move on from a relationship is never easy, but there are certain instances when a friend is over-the-moon thrilled to be free and when that happens, a congratulatory note is in order. Now is a perfect time to salute their courage and bravery.

Shannon,

It was fantastic to see you at Bonneview last week. Your positive perspective and optimistic outlook are life-affirming. Seriously. I can't wait to see all the good the world has in store for you.

I'm cheering you on!

Chelsea

How modern! In this day and age, couples are breaking the stereotypes of the bickering exes and choosing a path of respectful communication and mutual agreements. If they decide to share this news with you, why not commend them for their efforts to make big life changes in new and different ways? Your note should reflect the way they are presenting their new arrangement: If they would like to be seen as a united-yet-unmarried front, treat them as such. If they've made it clear they are embarking on their own paths, celebrate that decision.

Claire,

You two never cease to amaze me. The mutual admiration, care, and respect that you have brought to your conscious uncoupling is inspiring for all of us. I am wishing you both all the best in this new chapter.

Your biggest fan,
Jamie

apologies

stationery, boxed stationery, or a card

Nobody's perfect. We've all done or said things that we wish we could take back. That's where apologies come in. A sincere apology has the potential to clear the air and repair whatever damage has been done. You may even find that your relationship is better for it.

The biggest mistake when attempting an apology is using the word *but.* An apology is your moment to acknowledge your misstep—intentional or accidental—and following it up with the word *but* negates whatever came before it.

finding the

RIGHT WORDS

———

IT WAS WRONG OF ME TO . . .

NEXT TIME, I WILL . . .

YOU HAVE EVERY RIGHT TO FEEL
THE WAY YOU DO.

THERE'S NO EXCUSE.

I'M SORRY.

Carolyn,

I owe you a huge apology. Ever since
we saw each other last week, I have
been thinking about our conversation
and I can't believe how insensitive
I was. I wish I hadn't said a word.
Please know our friendship is
invaluable to me and that I would
never do anything to intentionally
cause you pain. I am truly sorry.

Always,
Chelsea

supplies

The key to keeping up with paper correspondence is being prepared. At the very minimum, keeping a few blank greeting cards and some stationery handy will ensure that you have what you need when you need it.

your stationery drawer

An artist needs their paints, a chef needs their ingredients, and a letter writer needs their supplies. The biggest consideration when assembling your stationery "drawer" is how often you write. If you're just getting started and hope to pop a birthday or thank you card in the mail occasionally, you can get by on the essentials. But if you plan on never missing a birthday, expressing your gratitude frequently, and becoming a master of the just-because note, you're going to want to stock up. Either way, remember to replenish regularly.

the
ESSENTIALS

―――

1 box of note cards

3 blank greeting cards with simple,
universal designs on the front

1 sheet of postage stamps

1 correspondence pen of your choice

. . .

the
CONNOISSEUR

―――

1 box of general note cards

1 set of personalized stationery with your name printed on it

A collection of greeting cards that you've collected over time

2 sheets of postage stamps with different designs
to match a mood or occasion

Several of your favorite pens so you're never
searching for the right one

Address book

TO OUR MOMS

Thank you for teaching us the importance of sending a handwritten note. You two believed in Sugar Paper first.

TO OUR DADS

Thank you for giving us the confidence to go after what we want in life.

TO OUR HUSBANDS

From the first coat of paint on our very first store, you both supported our vision when most people thought it was nuts. Thank you for loving us even when it's tricky.

TO OUR CHILDREN

You have grown up on Sugar Paper and always write your notes beautifully. One day you'll know why it matters so much.

TO THE SUGAR PAPER TEAM

Thank you for pouring your hearts into your work. Sugar Paper has always been a true collaboration.

TO CLARKSON POTTER

Thank you for keeping the tradition of the handwritten note alive by publishing this book.

TO AMANDA AND GABRIELLE

This book would not have happened without the two of you. Thank you for dotting every *i* and crossing every *t* with us.

TO IAN AND DANIELLE

Your art direction and illustrations brought the book to life.

TO EMILY, JOY, AND NICOLE

The endless hours spent making it look just right makes it look just right. Thank you for caring as much as we do.

TO CRYSTAL

Thank you for helping us find the words.

TO JAMESON

You made this book a priority because you knew it mattered. Thank you for keeping us on task.

TO OUR TRIBE

From the first women who walked into our store to the women we may never meet who make writing letters a priority. You are keeping the handwritten note alive one letter at a time.

A

address books, 21
  updating, 21
address on envelopes, 27–29
  centering, 28
  etiquette, 29
  how to, 28–29
  return, 28, 30
  titles, 28
adoptions, 70, 75
advanced degrees, 61
amicable separations, 129
anniversary cards, 45
apologies, 132
  finding the right words,
    133
  sample, 134
application letters, 101
  letters of
    recommendation, 106–7
  samples, 102–4

B

babies, 70–75
  finding the right words, 71
  new arrivals, 74
baby showers, 72
  sample, 73–74
ballpoint pens, 22
bereavement. See loss
birthdays, 48–55
  children, 50–52
  family, 54–55
  finding the right words,
    49
  friends, 53
  noting the milestone, 48
black color ink, 23
blank cards, 15
boxed stationery, 16, 139
business correspondence,
    91–107. See also
    educational endeavors;
    professional careers
  address on envelopes, 28
  finding the right words, 93
  letterhead for, 18
  letters for, 12
  personalized stationery
    for, 17
  professional holiday cards
    for, 88
  return addresses on, 30

C

cards
  about, 12
  types of, 15
card stock, 14

child. See also babies
  birthday cards, 50–52
  invitations and addressing
    envelope, 27
  loss of, 122
Christmas cards. See
    season's greetings
Cole, Henry, 86
collaborators, thank you
    notes for, 98–99
colleagues, thank you notes
    for, 98–99
college applications. See
    educational endeavors
college graduation, 61
condolence cards. See loss
conscious uncoupling, 131
cover letters, 18, 100

D

dating correspondence, 13
"dear" as salutation, 24
death of loved one. See loss
divorce. See separation and
    divorce

E

educational endeavors,
    100–107
  application letters, 101–4
  interview thank yous, 105
  letters of
    recommendation, 106–7
engagements, 62, 64
  finding the right words, 63
  sample, 65–66
envelopes, 26–30
  addressing an invitation,
    27, 29
  in boxed stationery, 16
  how to address an, 28–29
  for letterhead, 18
  postmarks, 31
  return addresses on,
    28, 30
  stamps, 31
exit letters from jobs, 97

F

family
  addressing envelope, 27
  birthday cards, 54–55
  loss of members, 123–25
  loss of pets, 125
  sign-offs, 24
felt tip pens, 23
fertility issues, 116
  sample, 117
"fondly" as sign-off, 24

formal invitations, address
    on envelopes, 29
formal sign-offs, 25
fountain pens, 23
friends
  addressing envelope, 27
  birthday cards, 53
  friendship letters, 46
  sample, 47

G

gifts
  for letters of
    recommendation, 106
  for new babies, 75
  thank you notes for, 36, 69
golden rules, 13
graduation, 56–61
  college and advanced
    degrees, 61
  finding the right words, 57
  high school, 58–60
grammar, 92
gratitude, thank you notes,
    38
  finding the right words, 35
  sample, 39
greeting cards, types of, 15

H

handwriting, 13
  for personal letters, 12
hardship, 112
  samples, 113–14
high school applications.
    See educational
    endeavors
high-school graduation, 58
  sample, 59–60
holiday cards, 82–89
  finding the right words, 83
  ink color, 23
  novelties, 84–85
  professional, 88
  return address on
    envelopes, 30
  samples, 89
  season's greetings, 86
  six easy steps for pulling
    off, 87
  stamps, 31
  updating address books
    for, 21
hosts, thank you notes
    for, 37

I

injury and illness, 115
ink color, 23

interviews. *See also* job
   interviews
school, thank you notes
   for, 105
invitations, address on
   envelopes, 27, 29

J
job interviews, 94
   samples, 95–96
joyful sign-offs, 25

L
letterhead, 18, 101
letters
   about, 12
   golden rules of, 13
   paper stock for, 14
letters of love, 40–47
   anniversaries, 45
   finding the right words, 41
   friendship, 46–47
   romance, 42–44
letters of recommendation,
   106
   sample, 107
liberating separations, 130
linen watermark paper, 18
loss, 118–25
   child, 122
   family member, 123–25
   finding the right words,
      119
   spouse or partner, 120–21
"love" as sign-off, 24, 25

M
marriage. *See* weddings
mentors, thank you notes
   for, 98–99
messy separations, 128
milestones, 76
   achievements, 81
   finding the right words, 77
   new home, 78–79
   new job, 80
   moving, 78
   sample, 79

N
new child. *See* babies
new home, 78
   sample, 79
new jobs, 80
New Year's cards, 87
novelty holiday cards, 84
   sample, 85

P
paper
   picking, 14
   types of, 15–18
partner, loss of, 120
   sample, 121
pencils, for adding names to
   address book, 21
pens, 22–23
personalized stationery, 17
pets, loss of, 125
photos, in holiday cards,
   86, 87
postmarks, 31
preprinted cards, 13, 15
professional careers, 92–99
   colleagues, collaborators,
      and mentors, 98–99
   the exit, 97
   finding the right words, 93
   interviews, 94–96
professional
   correspondence. *See*
   business correspondence
professional holiday cards,
   88
P.S. (postscriptum), 42

R
return addresses, on
   envelopes, 28, 30
rollerball pens, 22
romance, 42–44
   sample letters, 43–44

S
salutations, 24
school applications. *See*
   educational endeavors
school graduations, 58, 61
   samples, 59–60
season's greetings, 86
   finding the right words, 83
   professional cards, 88
   samples, 89
   six easy steps for pulling
      off, 87
separation and divorce,
   126–31
   amicable situation, 129
   conscious uncoupling, 131
   finding the right words,
      127
   liberating situation, 130
   thorny situation, 128
signature, including a
   sentiment with, 13
sign-offs, 24–25
   sample, 25

social correspondence,
   33–88. *See also* specific
   types of correspondence
   ink color, 23
   return address on
      envelope, 30
   spelling, 92
spouse, loss of, 120
   sample, 121
stamps, 31
stationery drawer, 138–39
   the connoisseur, 139
   the essentials, 139
Sugar Paper, 8–9
supplies, 137–39
support and sympathy,
   110–17. *See also* loss
   fertility issues, 116–17
   finding the right words,
      111
   hardship, 112–14
   injury and illness, 115

T
thank you notes, 34–39
   for colleagues,
      collaborators, and
      mentors, 98–99
   finding the right words, 35
   for gifts, 36
   gratitude, 38–39
   for hosts, 37
   for job interviews, 94–96
   for letters of
      recommendation, 106
   for school interviews, 105
   for wedding gifts, 69
thorny separations, 128
titles, on envelopes, 28
"tooth" of the paper, 14
traditional ink color, 23
traditional invitations,
   address on envelopes, 29
traditional sign-offs, 25
typed letters, 12

V
Valentine's Day cards, 84
   ink color, 23
   sample, 85

W
weddings, 62, 67
   finding the right words, 63
   sample, 68
wedding gifts, thank you
   notes for, 69
writing tools, 22–23

Published in the United States by Clarkson Potter/Publishers, an imprint of
Random House, a division of Penguin Random House LLC, New York.
clarksonpotter.com

CLARKSON POTTER is a trademark and POTTER with colophon is a
registered trademark of Penguin Random House LLC.

Library of Congress Cataloging-in-Publication Data
Names: Shukov, Chelsea, author. | Grobecker, Jamie, author.
Title: How to write a letter : find the words for every occasion / Chelsea
    Shukov and Jamie Grobecker.
Description: New York : Clarkson Potter/Publishers, [2021] | Identifiers:
    LCCN 2020046079 (print) | LCCN 2020046080 (ebook) | ISBN
    9781984825919 (Hardcover) | ISBN 9781984825919 (eBook)
Subjects: LCSH: Letter writing. | Social stationery.
Classification: LCC BJ2101.S548 2021 (print) | LCC BJ2101.S548 2021
    (ebook) | DDC 395.4--dc23
LC record available at https://lccn.loc.gov/2020046079
LC ebook record available at https://lccn.loc.gov/2020046080

ISBN 978-1-9848-2590-2
eISBN 978-1-9848-2591-9

Printed in China

Editor: Gabrielle Van Tassel
Production Editor: Serena Wang
Production Manager: Jessica Heim
Composition: Merri Ann Morrell and Nick Patton
Copy Editor: Laurie McGee
Indexer: Stephen Callahan

10 9 8 7 6 5 4 3 2 1

First Edition

Dear Reader,

Here we are at the end of the book. We hope we've made it a little easier for you to put pen to paper and send some love through the mail. You'll find that once you start writing, it will become a habit. If you ever want to practice, send us a note. We'll always write back. Promise.

With love,
Chelsea and Jamie